# ANIMALS UNDER THREAT

# GREY WOLF

**IN DANGER OF EXTINCTION!**

Jill Bailey

Heinemann

## www.heinemann.co.uk/library

Visit our website to find out more information about **Heinemann Library** books.

To order:
- ☎ Phone 44 (0) 1865 888066
- 🖹 Send a fax to 44 (0) 1865 314091
- 🖳 Visit the Heinemann Bookshop at www.heinemann.co.uk/library to browse our catalogue and order online.

First published in Great Britain by Heinemann Library, Halley Court, Jordan Hill, Oxford OX2 8EJ, part of Harcourt Education. Heinemann is a registered trademark of Harcourt Education Ltd.

Editorial: Patience Coster, Nicole Irving and Louise Galpine
Design: Ian Winton and Jo Hinton-Malivoire
Artwork: Stewart Lafford and Stefan Chabluk
Picture Research: Laura Durman
Production: Camilla Smith

Originated by Dot Gradations Ltd
Printed in China by WKT Company Limited

ISBN 0 431 18904 8 (hardback)
09 08 07 06 05
10 9 8 7 6 5 4 3 2 1

ISBN 0 431 18911 0 (paperback)
10 09 08 07 06
10 9 8 7 6 5 4 3 2 1

**British Library Cataloguing in Publication Data**
Bailey, Jill
Grey Wolf - (Animals in danger)
599.7'73
A full catalogue record for this book is available from the British Library.

## Acknowledgements

The Publishers would like to thank the following for permission to reproduce photographs: Ardea pp. **8** (Bill Coster/Ardea London), **40** (Mary Clay/Ardea London); Bruce Coleman Collection pp. **12** (Hans Reinhard), **13** (Bruce Coleman Inc.), **39** (Werner Layer); Corbis pp. **14** (Royalty-Free/Corbis), **23** (Peter Turnley), **25**, **26** (Hulton-Deutsch Collection), **28** (Bettmann), **29** (Layne Kennedy), **31** (Layne Kennedy), **32** (Lynda Richardson), **34** (Campbell William/Corbis Sygma); Frank Lane Picture Agency pp. **7** (S. Yoshino/Minden Pictures), **16** (A. Bardi/Panda Photo), **27** (G. Marcoaldi/Panda Photo), **41** (N. Biet/Panda Photo); Getty Images pp. **11**, **17** (both by Jim and Jamie Dutcher); International Wolf Centre (www.wolf.org) pp. **19** (Lynn and Donna Rogers - www.bearstudy.org), **33** (USFWS and Barron Crawford), **35**, **42**, **43**; Mary Evans Picture Library pp. **20**, **24**; NHPA pp. **5** (T. Kitchin and V. Hurst); Rolf O. Peterson pp. **30**, **37**; Still Pictures pp. **4** (Klein/Hubert), **36** (William Campbell), **38** (Peter Weimann); Team Husar.com pp. **10**, **18** (both by Lisa and Mike Husar). Cover photograph reproduced with permission of NHPA/David Middleton. Header image reproduced with permission of PhotoDisc.

The publishers would like to thank Michael Chinery assistance in the preparation of this book.

# Contents

Words printed in the text in bold, **like this**, are explained in the Glossary.

# The wild wolf

The grey wolf is the largest member of the dog family. Feared by many people yet admired by others as a symbol of the wilderness, it provokes strong emotions. It is a truly remarkable animal, able to survive in some of the most inhospitable places on Earth. Despite its fierce, even savage reputation, the grey wolf is a devoted parent. Wolf relatives share the care of the young and help older or weaker members of their group.

The grey wolf is a **predator**. It lives by hunting and eating other animals (prey). The prey ranges from large animals such as moose, bison (buffalo) and deer to smaller creatures such as hares, beavers and even mice. The type of prey available depends on the time of year and where the wolf lives. While some wolves live alone, most live in packs (groups). A pack of wolves can bring down prey as large as a bison, an animal ten times the weight of a single wolf. On some occasions, even a lone wolf may successfully kill a deer.

## Admired and hated!

Native Americans admire the wolf for its courage, cunning and survival skills. Many of their rituals have grown up using wolf symbols or skins. To them it is a natural part of the wilderness in which they live. On the other hand, most **ranchers** and reindeer herders hate the wolf. They **persecute** it because it kills their livestock and costs them money. Hunters see the wolf as a competitor to be eliminated. Farmers turn the wolf's habitat into fields, and cities and roads cover the wilderness in concrete.

*A wolf is the size of a large dog, measuring up to 81 centimetres (31 inches) at the shoulder and 2 metres (6.5 feet) from nose to the tip of its tail.*

Wolves live and hunt in packs. Most members of the pack belong to the same family. This pack is sharing a kill.

## A top dog

Grey wolves have few natural enemies. Their main enemy is humans. In some **habitats**, such as the northern forests of North America and Russia, they have formidable competitors like the brown bear, which may drive them off their kills and force them to spend more time hunting. But no animals deliberately hunt down and kill adult wolves.

In truly wild places, wolves can help to control the populations of their prey. Deer and moose populations tend to vary dramatically. When food is plentiful, and there are few or no predators, the populations increase rapidly. The plants they consume in such quantities are unable to grow back fast enough, so the animals start to run out of food. The population then crashes. Wolves tend to attack mainly sick and old animals, and the very young. This slows the rate of growth of the prey population and helps to prevent diseases spreading. By removing weak individuals so that they do not breed, wolves help to maintain a healthy stock of prey.

# Wolves worldwide

The wolf is one of the most widely distributed large **predators** in the world. It once roamed the entire northern hemisphere from the Arctic Ocean to Mexico. It was found in the Mediterranean, Arabia, India and Japan, in almost every **habitat**. The main prey of most wolves are large, hoofed, grazing mammals (ungulates) such as deer – for example, moose, elk and reindeer (caribou) – bison and antelopes. If they are to find enough prey to eat at all times of year, wolves must live in large, unspoiled, wilderness areas, such as forests, mountains, grasslands and the **tundra**.

Where human settlements come close to wolf territory, wolves also eat domestic livestock – for example, sheep, goats, cattle and even horses – as well as cats and dogs. The gradual spread of humans across the globe has brought people and their animals into conflict with wolves. It has also led to competition between humans and wolves to hunt animals, such as deer.

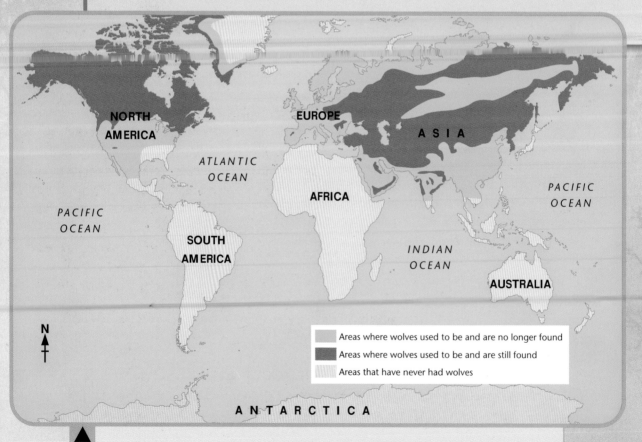

- Areas where wolves used to be and are no longer found
- Areas where wolves used to be and are still found
- Areas that have never had wolves

*This map shows the distribution of the grey wolf across the world today (in red) and in earlier times (in green). What it does not show is that while wolves may still survive in some places today, there are far fewer of them than there used to be.*

*Once there were vast areas of North America with millions of bison supporting thousands of wolves, but now scenes like this are a rare sight – the wolves and their prey have largely disappeared.*

# Wolves at war

Over the centuries, humans encroached on the wolf's natural habitat. The loss of habitat and prey made the wolves more likely to turn to sheep and cattle for food. Farmers, hunters and governments have mercilessly **persecuted** the wolf. This has drastically reduced numbers to the point where wolves have disappeared from large areas and become **extinct** in some countries. In others there remain only scattered lone wolves or pairs.

There are now scarcely any wild wolves in Germany and France, and none in the UK. The last UK wolves were hunted to extinction in Scotland in the middle of the 17th century. Many American states no longer have wolves. In densely populated parts of Asia, such as India, wolves are declining fast as their habitat disappears, and conflicts with expanding human populations become more frequent. In Scandinavia, numbers are so low that packs are rare, and many wolves live alone or in pairs.

## Fighting for territory

A wolf pack defends an area of land large enough to provide sufficient prey to support the pack and its offspring. This is called its territory. Usually a pack advertises its territory by means of scent marks and howling, so other wolves know to keep their distance. However, where wolf populations are expanding or where prey becomes scarce, encounters with neighbours are more frequent. The competing wolves become highly aggressive and fights often prove fatal. In the absence of humans, injuries from fights are the biggest cause of death among wolves.

# Different kinds of wolves

The grey wolf has a long history, dating back perhaps a million years. It is a species, which means that it is unlikely to breed with other kinds of wolves. Every species has a unique two-part Latin name – a **genus** name and a species name. The grey wolf belongs to the genus *Canis*, which also includes domestic dogs, jackals and coyotes. The grey wolf is *Canis lupus*.

Over long periods of time, populations on different continents or separated by large areas with no suitable **habitat**, gradually change. Those animals best suited to local conditions are more likely to survive and produce young. Eventually a population changes so much that it can no longer interbreed with other populations – it has become a new species. However, before it reaches this stage, it is known as a 'subspecies'.

## Wolf subspecies

There are about eleven subspecies of the grey wolf. They range from the large, heavy Alaskan/Canadian wolf to the small, slightly built Arabian wolf. The grey wolf is believed to have developed in Asia, from animal ancestors that migrated there from North America between one and two million years ago. It spread west to Europe, and probably crossed into North America about 300,000 years ago, when there was an ice bridge between the continents of Asia and North America across the Bering Sea.

A pack of coyotes surveys a flock of snow geese in New Mexico, USA. Many coyotes live alone, but some live and hunt in packs.

## Mixed-up species

Coyotes or prairie wolves (*Canis latrans*) were already in North America when the grey wolf arrived, as was another wolf, the dire wolf (*Canis dirus*). Coyotes, grey and dire wolves are all probably descended from a common ancestor. The coyote looks like a cross between a small wolf and a fox. On occasions the grey wolf and coyote may interbreed, forming **hybrids**.

## The mysterious red wolf

Scientists cannot decide whether the red wolf is a subspecies of the grey wolf, a species in its own right (*Canis rufus*), or a hybrid between the grey wolf and the coyote. Once common in the south-eastern United States, it was hunted almost to **extinction**. There are probably hardly any pure red wolves today, other than a few in captivity. **Genetic** evidence suggests that it may have been a separate species long ago, but has interbred with coyotes and grey wolves for thousands of years. The distinction is a vital one – if it is not a species, it is not protected by **conservation legislation**.

The dire wolf (now **extinct**) was a scavenger. It was the size of a large grey wolf, but had a broader head and shorter, sturdier legs. Its massive teeth were adapted for crushing bone. It could not run very fast and it probably lived rather like a hyena, feeding mainly on carcasses. It is believed to have fed on the remains of enormous grazing mammals, such as mammoths, and very large relatives of horses and deer. About 10,000 years ago, at the end of the last Ice Age, these large grazers disappeared, and with them the dire wolf.

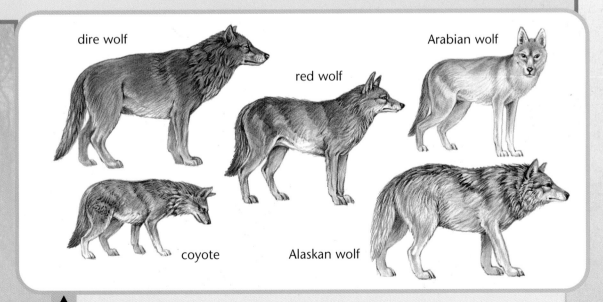

dire wolf

red wolf

Arabian wolf

coyote

Alaskan wolf

▲ *This illustration shows some of the different subspecies and hybrids of the grey wolf. The dire wolf is now extinct.*

# The wolf pack

The wolf pack is usually an extended family group. This generally consists of a breeding pair, their offspring and other non-breeding adults. Each wolf has its own rank within the pack, superior to some members and inferior to others. The breeding pair – the **alpha** male and female – is at the top of the pack and young or weaker wolves are at the bottom. Individuals vary greatly in size, physical strength and personality.

Dominant wolves are naturally bolder than lower-ranking animals, who may get bullied by the others. Wolves are highly competitive animals, and become aggressive when challenged. But they have developed an elaborate system of body positions, facial expressions and sounds that allows them to assess each other without fighting.

*These wolves are greeting the leader of the pack. The one on its back is giving a submissive display, to show the leader it respects his authority.*

## Territory

A wolf pack usually hunts over a particular area, called its territory. It defends this territory against other wolves, attacking them if they stray across its borders. By doing so the pack ensures it has a sufficient area over which to hunt to feed its members and their pups. The size of the territory depends on the size of the pack and the amount of available prey. The largest wolf pack on record contained 42 animals, but packs are usually much smaller than this. If there is plenty of prey available all year round, a territory as small as 33 square kilometres (13 square miles) may be enough to support a small pack.

Where prey is more scattered, a wolf pack may travel vast distances in the course of a year. The largest territory on record is several thousand square kilometres. In this case, the wolves lived in different parts of the territory at different times of the year. Wolves that follow migrating reindeer or antelope may cover an area greater than 100,000 square kilometres (over 38,000 square miles) during one year. This is not a true territory, however, because the wolves do not actively defend the whole **migration** route.

## Splitting up

If there are too many wolves in relation to the amount of prey, some may break away and form new packs elsewhere. If the wolves did not leave, the pack would have to defend a vast territory, and would spend too much time and energy travelling in search of prey. Neighbouring packs, especially those that are closely related, may join together in times of plenty and separate again when food becomes scarce.

## Lone wolves

A wolf is quite capable of surviving on its own. Many young wolves leave their family group to seek a mate and start a new pack or, on rare occasions, to join another pack. They may travel up to 800 kilometres (500 miles) in search of unoccupied territory. Older, low-ranking wolves may be driven from a pack by bullying. In Norway and Sweden, where there are very few wolves left, most live alone or in pairs. Lone wolves are also common in parts of the Middle East, where road-kill and livestock carcasses provide easily accessible food.

# Body of a hunter

The grey wolf's body is adapted for roaming and hunting over distance, and its long legs give it a loping stride. Like other dogs, the wolf walks on its toes rather than on the pads of its feet. This reduces friction and makes long-distance travel less tiring. The wolf's blunt claws enable it to grip and move easily over rocky ground.

Wolves can run at speeds of 64 kph (40 mph) but they cannot keep this up for long. They are best at loping along for mile after mile, covering up to 72 kilometres (45 miles) a day, at an average speed of about 8 kph (5 mph). They can also swim distances of up to 13 kilometres (8 miles), aided by small webs between their toes.

## Large and powerful

An average male wolf is almost as long as a human is tall, measuring between 1.5 and 2 metres from nose to tail tip, and between 66 and 81 centimetres in height at the shoulder. The female wolf is smaller. Desert wolves tend to be smaller than average, while the **tundra** wolves are the largest, powerful enough to bring down a large deer. A wolf may live for thirteen years in the wild, and up to seventeen in captivity.

### How to tell the age of a wolf

During its life, the wolf's tough diet of meat, skin and bones steadily wears down its teeth. By the time it reaches old age, the wolf's long, pointed, canine teeth may be half their original length, while its incisors may be worn right down to the roots. The enamel on the wolf's teeth grows thinner with age and the gums recede, exposing the base of each tooth. Scientists can therefore tell the age of a wolf by looking at its teeth.

A wolf is built for long-distance travel. It can patrol a sizeable area to secure a large enough supply of prey for its family.

*Wolves have a powerful sense of smell and acute hearing. They can detect sounds of higher pitch than humans can hear. Their eyes are particularly good at detecting movement.*

The wolf captures and kills its prey with its teeth. It has a long skull with massive jaws worked by powerful muscles, and its bite packs a pressure of 105 kilograms per square centimetre. The long, fang-like canine teeth near the front of the jaw help the wolf grip its prey and rip into flesh, and powerful, sharp-edged teeth called carnassials cut and shear flesh from bones. The teeth at the back of the mouth crack and crush bones. The smaller front teeth (incisors) jut out beyond the canines, so they can be used to grip, nip and pull at the flesh of both live and dead prey.

## Coat colour

The term 'grey' wolf is rather misleading. Grey wolves may be grey, black, cream or even pure white; some have beige or reddish coats. Pale wolves are most common in Arctic regions. Most wolves are a sort of mottled grey, but a single litter may contain pups of various colours. Like humans, wolves tend to become greyer with age.

# Communication

Wolves use a wide range of signals to communicate with each other. These signals help to reinforce the bonds between members of a pack. The wolves use them to communicate their emotions, identity and location, to warn of danger, to threaten and appease opponents and to assert their rank in the pack. Some Native Americans recognize more than 30 different wolf calls and howls.

A wolf that is uncertain about an approaching animal or strange noise may bark gently once or twice, perhaps to see if it gets a response. A series of loud, dog-like barks serves as a warning call, but a single bark can be an invitation to play.

Like dogs, wolves growl to threaten and warn off other animals. Pups growl in mock fights with other pups. Wolves greet each other with a series of yips and whines similar to the noises pups make while feeding.

## What's in a howl?

Wolves are famed for their howls, which have sent chills down the spine of many a traveller on a dark winter's night. A wolf pack howls together in a kind of ritual before setting out on a hunt. During a group howl, every wolf howls a different note. If two wolves start off on the same note, at least one will change note at once. This means a chorus of a few wolves can sound like a lot more, which will intimidate neighbouring packs. When wolves return from a hunt and are reunited with the rest of the pack there is often another round of howling to celebrate. Howls also help wolves make contact with each other in dense vegetation or over long distances.

*As in humans, each individual wolf has a different voice – a different howl. Nearby packs will answer so that all the wolves know their location and aggressive encounters are reduced.*

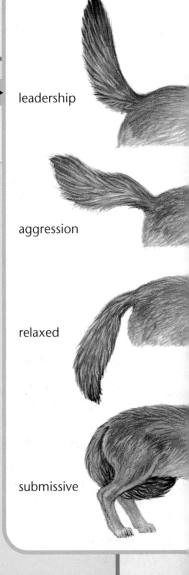

leadership

aggression

relaxed

submissive

You can tell a wolf's mood from the way it holds its tail.

# Secret signals

Wolves have an amazingly sensitive sense of smell. A wolf's sense of smell up to a hundred times more sensitive than that of humans. They can detect traces of scents 2 kilometres (1.5 miles) away. Wolves leave scent signals for other wolves to smell. As they travel, they urinate on objects, then scrape the ground with their paws to spread and pick up the scent. From this, other wolves can tell that the wolf has passed that way. The strength of the scent tells them how long ago this occurred and the direction in which the wolf was moving. Such signals also warn wolves when they are in another wolf pack's territory. Wolf droppings carry special scents, too.

Wolf scents tell other wolves who they are and to which pack they belong. They also carry other information. A female wolf's scent changes when she is ready to mate, and this may attract male wolves from some distance away. Scents also tell a wolf when there is prey near by, or if there is a carcass with flesh still on it, even if it is out of sight. Scents can carry long distances on the wind. Some warn of danger – it is useful for a wolf to know if there is a bear or a hunter around.

friendly

submissive

very aggressive

very defensive

Wolves use facial expressions to communicate.

# Pack power

The secret of the grey wolf's wide distribution and its survival against the odds is its **adaptability**. As well as having an astonishing sense of smell, the wolf can also detect sounds up to 16 kilometres (10 miles) away. These qualities, together with the ability to see at night, mean that it can hunt around the clock. Working in a pack, wolves are capable of bringing down prey such as bison, moose and musk oxen. These animals are ten times the size of an individual wolf. Wolves can also survive on a diet of mice and carrion (dead flesh). A wolf may consume 9 kilograms of meat at a single sitting, then go for weeks without eating.

Wolves take advantage of the seasons. They hunt calves and fawns (young deer) in spring, male moose, male bison and stags (male deer) in the autumn (when the males are weakened by the **rut**), and old and very young animals in the winter, when the prey is weakened by cold and lack of food. Wolves have also been known to fish for salmon. They wade in and herd the fish into shallow pools, where they are trapped and easy to catch. Alternatively, a wolf may hunt from the riverbank, plunging its long, narrow snout in to grab the fish.

▲ A particularly large pack of wolves sets out to hunt on a snowy Italian mountainside.

## Wolf and prey

A pack of wolves disturbs a large moose, which takes to its heels. The wolves give chase. The moose stops and turns to face them. The wolves pull up and keep their distance, watchful and wary – eventually they move away. Even smaller animals may be left alone if they stand their ground. But sick animals often make no attempt to flee or defend themselves, so providing an easy source of food for wolves.

*A wolf pack gathers for the hunt. The wolves' large paws help them stay on top of the snow, but deep snow can weaken prey animals such as deer as they try to wade through it.*

# Hunting strategy

Wolves capture small prey easily by stalking and pouncing, but hunting large prey is a dangerous business. Wolves can die or get seriously maimed as a result of a kick from an elk or moose or by a thrust of its antlers. Wolves use teamwork to distract the prey. Some attack its **flanks** while others seize its head and neck, biting and clinging, even dangling from it. A common tactic is to seize the nose until the prey starts to suffocate and sinks to its knees. Even weak members of the pack play a part: old wolves may have expert tracking skills and a good memory of the territory.

The secret of the wolf's hunting prowess is its stamina – it can pursue prey relentlessly, sometimes for hours, until the victim tires. Wolves usually stalk their prey for many kilometres, assessing them, looking for weaklings and stragglers. Often they make a mock attack, then withdraw, testing the prey's readiness to fight back or flee. Repeated challenges may force the prey to flee, revealing the slow and weak. Wolves chase far more animals than they actually attack. Even when they do attack, their success rate may range from one in ten to one in 25, or worse.

# Bringing up the young

In most wolf packs, only the **alpha** male and female breed. They prevent others from breeding by threats and bullying. If prey is particularly plentiful, a second pair may be allowed to breed. In this way, wolves regulate the size of the pack so that it does not run out of food.

The female wolf becomes receptive to mating only once a year, for 5-14 days during the period from late January to early March or April, and her pregnancy lasts for about nine weeks. There is a lot more aggression around mating time, as the wolves seek to establish and maintain their rank in the pack. Young and low-ranking wolves often grow tired of being bullied and having to wait till last when feeding at a kill, and decide to leave the pack.

Snuggling up for warmth and safety, these wolf cubs will feed on their mother's milk for at least five weeks. The pack stays near by to protect the female and her cubs.

## A family affair

All the wolves help dig a den for the female to give birth in. This is usually a hole in the ground, but a hollow log or cave may be used instead. The young are born in spring, when the animals that wolves prey upon produce young, too, and food is plentiful. While the pups are very tiny, the pack stays in the area around the den. Wolf pups are born helpless, blind and deaf. They rely on their mother's milk until they are about five weeks old. Then they are fed on half-digested meat regurgitated by the adults. Most members of the pack help to guard and feed the young.

At about one month old, the pups emerge from the den and start to explore the world. They ask for food from adults by licking and nuzzling their faces. When they are about ten weeks old, their mother moves them, often to an open place such as a meadow close to water. By now the pups are old enough to run and hide when danger threatens.

## Moving on

At about four months old, the pups are strong enough to accompany the adults to kills. In the autumn they start to follow the hunt, putting into practice skills they began to learn through play. Now the pack can move on to elsewhere in its territory area. At one year old, the young are fully grown. They may stay in the pack for up to three more years, refining their hunting skills and helping to care for new brothers and sisters, or they may leave the pack, perhaps to find a mate and start a pack of their own.

## The importance of play

Pups love to play. They stalk each other, chase and pounce, and paw at one another's faces. But this is not just play – they will need these skills for the hunt later in their lives. Through play they learn the gestures vital for socializing with other wolves – bows, tail-wags, aggressive and submissive postures. In games like tag, keep away, play-wrestling and king-of-the-castle they learn to interact with other wolves and develop long-lasting social bonds. The exercise also helps their muscles to grow and improves their co-ordination.

▶

*Play is an important part of growing up, helping to build the strong muscles and quick responses that will be needed in the hunt.*

Although a wolf may live for up to thirteen years, many never reach that age. Before they become old enough to suffer the diseases of old age, such as cancer, **arthritis**, heart and kidney disease, most wolves will die. Many wolves are injured or killed by hunters and farmers. Traps and snares set for other animals can also capture and injure a wolf, who may even bite off a foot to escape. Some die from injuries sustained during the hunt or in fights with other wolves. Young wolves learning to hunt are particularly vulnerable, because they are weak, and inexperienced at steering clear of horns and hooves.

Adult wolves are remarkably resilient – they can survive broken ribs from the kick of a deer, and even skull fractures and broken legs. Sometimes, however, wounds become infected, and **gangrene** may set in. Wolves with limb deformities are less able to hunt and, unless the pack supports them, they become weakened by hunger and susceptible to disease. Older wolves often suffer arthritis in damaged joints.

*This dramatic illustration shows an Italian woman snatching her child away from the jaws of a large wolf. When wolves are suffering from rabies, they may attack and bite humans. Such attacks are extremely rare.*

## Rabies

For centuries, humans have had a great fear of wolf attacks, and the wolf has been persecuted as a result. Tales of frenzied attacks, especially from Europe in earlier times, have helped to increase the wolf's fearful reputation. Most of the fatal attacks that have been investigated were by wolves or wolf-dog **hybrids** suffering from rabies. This virus affects the brain, causing the animal to become listless. It produces lots of saliva, and repeatedly bites other animals and even lifeless objects. Rabies is passed from animal to animal in the saliva of bites. It can be passed from dogs and wolves to humans, and is often fatal.

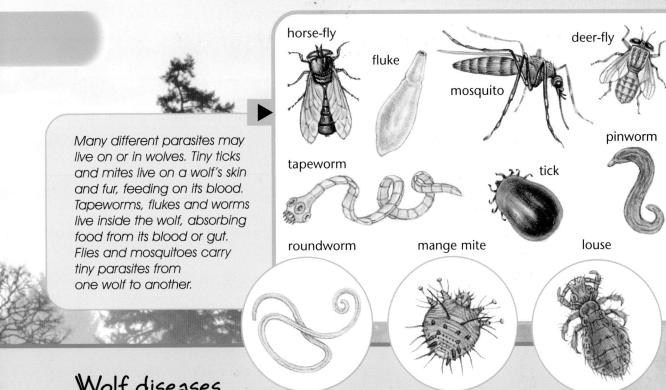

horse-fly
fluke
mosquito
deer-fly
pinworm
tapeworm
tick
roundworm
mange mite
louse

*Many different parasites may live on or in wolves. Tiny ticks and mites live on a wolf's skin and fur, feeding on its blood. Tapeworms, flukes and worms live inside the wolf, absorbing food from its blood or gut. Flies and mosquitoes carry tiny parasites from one wolf to another.*

## Wolf diseases

Many of the diseases caused by viruses and bacteria that affect domestic dogs are also a danger to wolves. Such diseases include rabies (see box opposite), **distemper** and **canine parvovirus**. In the wild, contact with other wolf packs is limited, but as more humans move to wilderness areas or visit them for recreation, wolves come into increased contact with domestic dogs and are at risk of picking up infections to which they have no natural resistance.

## Parasites

Many tiny animals live on and inside wolves. Parasites such as lice, fleas, ticks and mites hide in their fur and feed on their blood and tissues. If there are a lot of parasites, the wolf may become tired, or may be so distracted by itching and scratching that it does not catch enough prey. **Mange** mites can cause the wolf to lose much of its fur, making it susceptible to the cold and to other skin infections. Other external parasites, such as deer-flies, horse-flies, black-flies and mosquitoes, steal a quick meal of blood and move away, but their saliva may transmit viruses and other diseases.

Inside the wolf is another assortment of unwanted creatures – tapeworms, roundworms, **hookworms** and **flukes**. Tapeworms and roundworms live in the wolf's intestine, absorbing already digested food through their skins. They release millions of tiny eggs, which pass out in the wolf's droppings, to be picked up by other animals. Wolves become infected when they eat one of these animals. A heavy load of internal parasites may make a wolf more susceptible to infectious diseases.

# Wolves and humans

The earliest drawings of wolves are in caves in southern Europe, and date from 20,000 BC. In those far-off days humans lived in small communities much like wolves, sheltering in caves and hunting grazing mammals. There was plenty of prey, so wolves had no reason to attack humans, and humans had no reason to **persecute** wolves.

Some time around 5000 BC or even earlier, humans began to settle down, to develop agriculture and herd livestock. From this point on, everything changed. Wolves were deprived of their natural **habitat** and prey by human farming methods and forest clearance. They therefore began to attack livestock which, after all, looked very much like their natural prey.

*Long ago, humans lived in small groups and hunted their prey alongside wolves. In the picture below, humans and wolves are hunting bison.*

## Attacks on humans – fact or fiction?

Most of the time wolves avoid humans, slipping quietly away when they approach. Unless a pack of wolves is starving, a single shepherd can usually drive it off. Humans are not the wolf's natural prey. But fear of wolf attacks increased dramatically in Europe as the human population grew and moved into wolf territory. Until about 200 years ago, rabies was common in Europe. A **rabid** wolf will attack humans – and any other animal. But far more common are attacks by large dogs and wolf-dog **hybrids**, which are often mistaken for true wolves. In the last 50 years, no one has been killed by wolves in North America. Only seven people in the whole of Europe and Russia have been killed. This is far fewer than the number of annual deaths from motor vehicles or even from falling off horses.

▶

*Some Native Americans used to cover themselves in wolf skins as a disguise to get close to animals they were hunting. This ceremonial Comanche outfit includes a wolf-skin head-dress.*

# Spirit power

Some cultures, such as the Nunamiut Inupiat of Alaska and the Celts and Anglo-Saxons of Britain, continued to see wolves as a natural part of their environment. They admired the wolves' prowess in hunting, and human hunters and heroes often took wolf names, for example, Rudolf (from Ruhm-wolf, meaning 'victorious wolf' in Norse language). Hunting and healing rituals developed involving wolves, wolf skins and wolf bones.

Wolves were thought to have spiritual and healing powers. The Alaskan Tanaina believed wolves were once men, and saw them as brothers, providing food (in the form of carcasses) for other animals such as foxes, coyotes and ravens. The Japanese word for wolf means 'great god'. Until the 19th century, Japanese people saw wolves as allies. Wolves killed the deer and other animals that damaged and ate people's crops.

Legend claims that a female wolf brought up the twins Romulus and Remus, the founders of Rome. Other tales of humans brought up by wolves are surprisingly common in Europe and Russia. Some may have arisen when small children wandered off and found a wolf's den. There are a few authentic records of wolves allowing tiny children to mingle with their pups without harming them.

# An unreasonable fear

While hunters may have respected and admired the wolf, **nomads** who wandered the wilderness with their flocks of sheep and goats saw the wolf as an enemy. The Greek storyteller Aesop, who lived in the 6th century BC, wrote fables describing the cunning and deceit of the wolf.

In this early 20th-century illustration, a werewolf returns home from a night on the prowl.

## Enemy of the gods

According to legend, the Greek god Apollo took on the form of a wolf to fight, but he was also known as the wolf-slayer. In **Nordic** legends, Odin, ruler of the gods, had two wolves always beside him. It was said that the end of the world would come when Skoll and his brother Hati, two giants disguised as wolves who fed on the bones of murderers and adulterers, finally devoured the Sun and the Moon. At this time the giant wolf, Fenris, would be set loose to attack and kill Odin and the gods.

## Werewolves

From at least the time of Christ, Europe's hatred of the wolf found expression in the **persecution** of so-called werewolves – people who were said to turn into wolves by night, often at certain stages of the moon. This fear became widespread in the Middle Ages, and persists in remote parts of Russia to this day. Werewolves were supposed to have made a pact with the devil, or to have been turned into werewolves as a punishment for sinning. Churches had great power in those days, and great influence on the laws of the land. The church exploited people's fears in a bid to gain more supporters. Clerics denounced werewolves from the pulpit and put pressure on local law-makers to criminalize them. Many people were executed for a crime called lycanthropy (being werewolves).

▲ *Wolves feature as a sinister presence in many old legends and fairy tales. In the story pictured, a wolf eats the little girl's (Red Riding Hood's) grandmother. The animal then puts on its victim's clothes in order to trap the child.*

The Bible was written in a land where many people guarded their flocks of sheep and goats against wolves. The Bible tended to use wolves as a symbol of cunning and deceit, but the shepherds did not see them as particularly bad. Later Christian teaching increasingly used the wolf as a symbol of evil. It taught that humans were put on Earth to become masters over the animals, and this contributed to the changing attitude towards wolves.

## Pact with the devil

By the Middle Ages (AD 500 1500), the wolf was feared as an agent of the devil and an enemy of humans. Ancient associations of the wolf with the supernatural now increased people's fears. Even traditional children's tales such as *Red Riding Hood* and *The Three Little Pigs* have the wolf as the villain.

Times were hard, and people looked for something to take out their frustrations on. Governments ordered wolf hunts, sometimes compelling thousands of people to take part. Packs of starving stray dogs were common at the time, and so was rabies. Unprovoked attacks by large **rabid** dogs were often attributed to wolves, further fuelling people's fears.

# Persecution!

European **migrants** took their fear of wolves with them to North America. At one time, the **prairies** supported some 80 **billion** bison – a source of food for wolves and Native American people alike. But when the Europeans arrived, they hunted the bison mercilessly, not just for food but for pleasure, until the vast herds were brought to the brink of **extinction**.

To make matters worse for the wolf, the migrants turned over much of its former wilderness home of grassland and forest to growing wheat and rearing livestock. This agricultural revolution deprived the wolves of hunting territory and natural prey. New railways and long-distance **cattle drives** brought in new kinds of food for wolves, increasing the conflict between humans and wolves.

This new breed of human hunters, armed with deadly firearms, saw wolves as thieves and competitors to be destroyed. Even today in Canada and Alaska, when hunters kill so many deer that their numbers fall dramatically, they blame the wolves and have them shot, too.

## A price on its head

For thousands of years, kings and governments, and later **ranchers**, have paid wolf bounties (money for killing wolves). In the 10$^{th}$ century, King Edgar of England allowed people to pay their taxes in wolf heads and their fines in wolf tongues. Bounty hunting continues today in Russia, where the government offers rewards for wolves killed outside nature reserves, and in Kazakhstan, where it is claimed that some 60,000 wolves kill 175,000 sheep, goats, calves and camels a year.

*In this photo from the mid-20th century, American bounty hunters count the bodies of wolves they have just slain. Each dead wolf would have fetched a $35 bounty payment.*

Between 6000 and 7000 wolf skins are traded across the world each year, supplied mainly by Russia, Mongolia and China. The fur is used to trim parka jackets.

In the USA, bounty hunting led to the slaughter of wolves on an unprecedented scale. The first American bounty was offered by the Massachusetts Bay Colony in 1630. Between 1850 and 1900, more than a million wolves were killed in the USA. Wolf skins also fetched good prices.

## The bounty hunter

A typical 14th-century bounty hunter worked on the railways, in mines or on ranches in summer, and hunted wolves in winter. In the afternoon he shot bison and laced the carcasses with poison. Next morning he returned to pick up the dead animals that had fed on the meat. The journal of a pair of bounty hunters who shared a camp in Kansas, USA, in the winter of 1862 records that they killed 800 wolves, more than 2000 coyotes and 100 foxes, netting themselves $2500 – a princely sum in those days.

## Killed for conservation

To make matters worse, from 1915 to 1942, the US Biological Survey, Department of Fish and Wildlife and national parks managers also killed wolves to protect the herds of deer and other game animals. This activity occurred particularly in Colorado, Wyoming, Montana, the Dakotas, Arizona and New Mexico. Wolves were poisoned, trapped, and even shot from aeroplanes, despite the fact that wolves and game had co-existed for thousands of years without either becoming extinct.

Bounty payments in the USA stopped in 1965. But by the time the **Endangered Species** Act of 1973 finally gave the wolf protection, only a few hundred were left in the USA except for in Alaska. Times have finally changed: in the USA today you will be rewarded for killing a wolf not with a bounty, but with a $100,000 fine and a year in jail!

# Top predator brought down

Humans have used every means at their disposal to kill wolves. In India, simple pit traps are used, disguised with branches or leaves. The wolves fall in and people then stone them to death. Early hunters used bows and arrows, then guns. A common method was to wait for parents to leave the pups, then raid the den, kill the pups, and shoot the parents as they returned.

▲ An American hunter returns to a leg trap to find a dead wolf caught by its paw. Such traps catch many other animals indiscriminately, and could seriously injure humans, too.

Trappers who wanted to sell wolf skins did not want bullet holes in them, so they used steel leg-hold traps. These traps do not distinguish between wolves and other animals, so any creature unfortunate enough to step on one was trapped, maimed and often left to starve to death. Coyotes, foxes, bears, mountain lions (also called pumas or cougars), **wolverines**, European lynx, humans and dogs have all been caught in these traps. Leg-hold traps are now illegal in Europe, but they are still used elsewhere.

## Poisoned and pursued

Poisoned carcasses have also been used to kill wolves. The use of **strychnine** is now illegal in many places, but rat poison is still used. Poisoned carcasses also kill many natural scavengers such as bears, coyotes, foxes, wolverines, jackals, vultures, ravens and crows.

In 1909 the US state of Montana even tried a kind of biological control, ordering its vets to capture wolves and infect them with **mange**, so that it would spread to other wolves. This was an incredibly reckless policy because mange can also infect other game species, domestic livestock and dogs.

In some places hounds have been used to pursue and corner wolves and other **predators**, which are then shot. Today, wolves are pursued across open country in planes or helicopters and shot from the air. In parts of the Russian **tundra**, aerial hunting has driven the tundra wolf into the forest, where it has bred with another subspecies, the Eurasian wolf.

In Minnesota, USA, in 1998, an American government worker sets a wolf trap close to a cow carcass that has been laid out as bait.

## After-effects

When wolves are removed from an area, their former prey – deer – usually multiplies until it outgrows the local food supply. Then, in a hard winter, the animals starve to death in great numbers. The local vegetation is destroyed by overgrazing and may take years to grow back, removing a food supply for rodents and many other small mammals and birds that feed on plants or their seeds. If wolves are not removed from an area, there is much less of a fluctuation in the population. In places where the wolf has been removed, other predators increase unless they, too, are killed by poison or traps laid for the wolves. But without the wolf leftovers, scavenging animals are deprived of easy meals.

## A wolf scientist

In 1939, Adolph Murie conducted the first scientific study of wolves. He was employed to help the Mount McKinley Park Service in Alaska plan their future management, and he investigated the relationship between wolves and their prey (mostly mountain sheep and caribou). To most people's surprise, he discovered that wolves and prey are usually in balance, and that wolves prey mainly on sick, old and very young animals. By removing the sick they help maintain the health of the prey population, and they also prevent it outgrowing its food supply. This means that the prey does not suffer mass starvation and dramatic falls in population. This was the start of a big change in public opinion about the wolf in North America.

# The wolves of Isle Royale

Isle Royale is an island on Lake Superior in Michigan, USA. In 1949, during a severe winter an ice bridge to the mainland formed and a pair of unrelated wolves from Ontario crossed it. They found lots of moose and no humans, and began to breed there. In 1958, Durward Allen began a study of these wolves, and his young Ph.D. student, David Mech, took it up in 1959. The study continues to this day, with the aid of volunteers from all over the world.

*A moose is tracked by wolves across a snowy landscape on Isle Royale on the US/Canadian border. Aerial surveys are important in assessing the numbers of wolves and their prey.*

## A good influence?

Until the wolves arrived, the moose population on Isle Royale had followed the pattern of extreme fluctuation – first becoming too numerous, then overgrazing and dying of malnutrition. With the arrival of the wolves, the population stabilized, and fluctuations became less extreme. Many moose produced twins and their reproduction rates rose, so they were obviously very healthy. This demonstrated that **predator** and prey are more or less in balance in the long term – and that the presence of wolves does not necessarily reduce the numbers of moose and other prey. This discovery had a great influence on public attitudes to the wolf and helped persuade the government to reduce its slaughter.

At first Mech found that the wolves killed mainly the very young, old or diseased moose. But in the 1970s they began to take moose of prime breeding age. Coping with the deep snow of a severe winter had weakened the moose. By 1980, after three harsh winters, there were 50 wolves in several packs – one wolf every 8 square kilometres (3 square miles), twice the highest wolf density ever recorded. As a result, the moose population fell dramatically.

## A new puzzle

In the early 1980s many of the wolves caught **canine parvovirus** from dogs taken illegally to the island. By 1982 only 15 wolves survived. In 1988 the wolf population on Isle Royale fell again, and by 1993 there were only twelve left. No pups were born for several years, despite the highest-ever density of moose. As the moose population increased to 2400 animals in 1995, there were still only 15 wolves on the island.

For a decade after the virus was eliminated, the wolves did not recover. A cause for this may have been lack of **genetic** diversity. If animals (including humans) repeatedly breed with close relatives, they become less fertile, have less resistance to disease and suffer high infant mortality. Scientists feared the Isle Royale wolves might not recover, but in 1996 they began to breed again, and by the year 2000 there were 29. Clearly, there is still much to learn about the interactions between wolves and their environment.

## The Magic Pack moves in

In November 1985 a very special event took place. A pack of twelve wolves, the Magic Pack (so named because it has a tendency to disappear for long periods and then suddenly reappear), crossed the border from British Columbia in Canada, where wolves are protected, into Montana's Glacier National Park in the USA. The following spring they produced the first pups to be born in the western USA for more than 50 years. Since then, their descendants have multiplied and formed several packs. Although the pack's increase has coincided with an upsurge of public sympathy towards the wolf, many of these wolves have been shot, trapped or poisoned.

*The world famous wolf expert David Mech carries an anaesthetized wolf back to camp, where scientists will measure it and investigate its state of health.*

# Captive wolves

Many **endangered species** have been saved by captive breeding. This involves rearing the animals in captivity. If captive populations become large enough, attempts may be made to reintroduce some of the animals into the wild where large enough areas of suitable **habitat** remain. Wolves are not easy to keep in captivity. Ideally they need a large area in which to roam. Unrelated wolves that are thrust together may go through a stressful and violent struggle to sort out their dominance relationships.

## On the brink of extinction

In 1967 the red wolf was declared an endangered species, and by the 1970s it was almost **extinct** in the wild. Unable to find mates of their own species, many red wolves had taken to mating with coyotes, and pure-blooded red wolves were disappearing. Only a few remained in Texas and Louisiana. The US Fish and Wildlife Service found only fourteen pure-blooded red wolves among the 400 remaining animals, and between 1974 and 1979 these were sent to a breeding centre at a zoo in Washington state. Some of the offspring of the fourteen red wolves that bred were taken to other breeding centres across the USA.

Collars emitting radio signals were fastened on to the wolves to track them upon their reintroduction into the wild. Captive-bred red wolves were released on to Bulls Island off the coast of South Carolina, where human contact was reduced to a minimum. For the first few months carcasses were left for them to ensure they had enough food. But would they still have the necessary hunting and survival skills?

*Animal handler Don Bailey socializes with two captive grey wolves at a wolf park in Indiana, USA. Such parks are used to breed wolves in the hope of introducing them to the wilderness areas that have lost their wolf populations.*

A red wolf pictured at the International Wolf Centre in Minnesota, USA. Captive breeding and reintroduction into wilderness areas is helping to save the endangered red wolf.

## Success story

The wolves did well, and in 1987 the first pair was released at the Alligator River National Wildlife Refuge in North Carolina. By 1993 some 30 red wolves were breeding there. In 1991 more were released in the Great Smoky Mountains National Park in Tennessee, and other reserves. By 2003 more than 280 pups had been born in the wild – for the time being, the red wolf was out of danger.

The Mexican wolf, the smallest and most southerly North American wolf subspecies that once roamed the oak woodlands of Arizona, New Mexico, Texas and Mexico, appears to be extinct in the wild. In 1980, the last five individuals were caught to start a captive-breeding programme. Since 1998, small numbers of captive-bred Mexican wolves have been released in Arizona and New Mexico. By late 2002, there were 28 wolves in the wild in eight packs.

## Wolf-dog hybrids

Wolf lovers and people wanting a status symbol are often tempted to keep wolves or wolf-dog **hybrids** as pets. Many of these animals are later abandoned to wolf refuges. It took thousands of years to breed the domestic dog species from the wild wolf, and evolution cannot be repeated in a few months. Even a wolf-dog cross that contains equal amounts of **genetic** material from each parent may be more wolf-like than dog-like. Wolf lovers beware – most so-called wolf attacks on humans are made by wolf-dog hybrids. Domesticated wolves lose their fear of humans, but keep their natural instincts to chase prey that runs. Dogs, cats and small children may trigger this instinct, with fatal consequences. Wolves do not make good guard dogs either – they are naturally wary of the unfamiliar and will hide from visitors rather than bark at them.

# The Yellowstone wolves

This wolf has been caught in a net fired from a helicopter in Yellowstone National Park. It will be fitted with a radio collar so that its movements can be tracked, then it will be re-released.

Now that public opinion is turning in favour of the wolf, attempts are being made to return it to some of its former haunts. The most obvious problems arising from this are the wolf's tendency to kill livestock, its effect on the livelihoods of local farmers, and opposition from hunters. In 1982 the US government amended the **Endangered Species** Act to allow reintroduced wolves to be designated as 'experimental' rather than 'endangered'. This permits **ranchers** to kill problem animals that threaten human life or wipe out livestock on their own land, and also provides for permits to cull wolves in similar circumstances on public lands. When necessary, problem wolves may be trapped and moved to other areas.

One of the earliest reintroductions was at Yellowstone National Park in the north-western USA. Yellowstone is a large area of mountains, forests, grasslands and lakes. Wolves were deliberately eliminated from the park in the 1920s to protect the large herds of elk and other herbivores. The elk then thrived to the point where they were destroying large areas of vegetation.

After twenty years of heated public consultation, campaigns by wolf support groups and various legal actions, 31 grey wolves from Canada were released into Yellowstone in 1996. This was a 'soft release' programme, with the wolves first held in pre-release pens, where it was hoped they would bond and form packs (lone wolves are more likely to wander far from the release site). Each wolf released was fitted with a radio collar and its movements were tracked.

By early 2002, Yellowstone and the surrounding area had 250 wolves in 28 packs. But by then the wolves had killed some 97 cattle and 426 sheep, and 59 wolves had been destroyed because they repeatedly preyed on livestock. This was actually far fewer than had been predicted. Nevertheless, there is still hostility toward the wolves from local ranchers.

At Yellowstone, the group Defenders of Wildlife funded a compensation scheme for ranchers. While compensation schemes help reduce hostility, claims can be hard to prove. Wolves quickly devour all their kills, and also eat animals that have died from other causes. Of the $12 million already spent by 'Operation Wolfstock' to return wolves to Yellowstone and also to central Idaho, a significant proportion is made up of compensation claims and legal fees.

*Visitors enjoying a 'public wolf howl' at the International Wolf Centre in Minnesota, USA. If they are lucky, the centre's resident wolves will howl back.*

# Eco-tourism

Without public support, wolf recovery programmes will fail. One of the best ways to win over the public is to give people the opportunity to see wolves. **Eco-tourism** – where tourists visit places to see wildlife – is promoted by wolf refuges, where displaced wild wolves or unwanted pets end up, and by parks and reserves where wolves have been reintroduced. Public howls are popular – experienced staff mimic wolf howls, and the real wolves howl back. Exhibitions, TV programmes, talks, wolf information and activity centres, wolf-watching holidays and wolf merchandise all help to improve the wolf's image. They also raise money for **conservation** and provide jobs and income for the local community.

Working with wolves is an energetic business. It can consist of long wilderness treks, carrying camping gear and bags full of deer bones. Studying wolf behaviour involves spending long periods with a particular wolf pack in a hide close to the breeding den or rest area. Or it can mean watching wolves at a distance with a powerful telescope or binoculars and following them on foot. Wolves leave very distinctive footprints on the ground and in snow.

Scientists study the relationships between wolves and their prey (including livestock) to assess the impact of wolves in a particular area. Wolf territories can cover hundreds of square kilometres, so scientists often survey the area by plane or helicopter (by plane is quieter) to locate the pack.

## Radios for wolves

Wolves are often fitted with radio collars transmitting signals that can be picked up by a hand-held radio receiver. The wolves are first trapped, either by shooting tranquillizing darts into them (often done from low-flying planes), or by driving them into nets (this is more distressing for the wolves). Some radio collars transmit signals to satellites orbiting the Earth, so scientists can follow the wolves' movements on a computer. Scientists may also inject a chemical into a wolf, which will show up in its droppings for some time afterwards.

Analysis of wolf droppings shows the kinds of food a wolf has eaten and any diseases it might have. It also helps scientists discover which individuals are killing livestock, for example.

*A wolf is fitted with a radio collar.*

*The radio signals emitted by the collar can be picked up by a hand-held aerial, so scientists can tell where a wolf is without having to follow it on the ground.*

If the scientists get the chance to follow the pack, they record the frequency with which the wolves attack, how often they succeed in killing their prey, and the age and sex of the prey. A lot can be learned without ever catching sight of a wolf. Scientists look for the remains of animals killed by wolves. Any kills seen from the air are later investigated on the ground. Blood on the ground or snow, tracks relating to a chase, or signs of a struggle all suggest a wolf attack.

## Reading the past

From the animal tracks and remains, the scientists can find out information about the prey population. For example, the skeleton of a ten-year-old moose that died in 2002 indicates that it was alive in 1992. By combining this data with aerial surveys of prey populations, scientists can calculate the size and age structures of populations in earlier years. All this information is put together to get a complete record of wolf and prey numbers, movements and kills.

### Old bones

Once they find a kill, the scientists remove bones for measuring later. The lower jaws and teeth provide clues to the prey's age at death, and the leg bones, hips and back can be checked for **arthritis** and other diseases. The marrow fat indicates how fit the prey was; and the skull size (brain volume) provides clues to how the animal was affected by nutrition early in life.

# Saving European and Russian wolves

The **tundra**, northern forests and grassy plains of Russia and its neighbouring countries are so vast that many wolves still live there. In Russia, Mongolia and China, hunters trap thousands every year for their fur and there is also some trapping in parts of Canada, where the fur is used mainly to trim parkas. No one knows how many wolves remain in the vast wilderness areas of China, Mongolia and Central Asia. Even here, wolves are losing their prey to human hunters. In just ten years, 90 per cent of the **saiga antelopes** of the Central Asian **steppes** have been killed for their horns, which are used in Eastern medicine. The loss of such an important prey means that wolves are more likely to kill livestock or enter urban areas to feed on rubbish.

## The Downtown Pack

In the Carpathian Mountains of Romania, a radio-collared wolf pack, nicknamed the Downtown Pack, scavenges in the town of Brasov at night, and calmly walks back out of town during the morning rush hour. In Eastern Europe, wolves scavenging in cities interbreed with local stray dogs. The **hybrid** offspring are aggressive and dangerous. Where human campers and hikers leave food lying around, this leads to more unwelcome encounters with wolves – and bears. There have been some attacks on people, especially children.

*A pack of wolves howls in a wintry German forest. Howling is a good way to communicate over long distances, in dense forest or at night. Each wolf has a different howl.*

*An Irish wolfhound, once called a wolfdog, is the tallest breed of dog. It was bred almost 2000 years ago to hunt wolves and elk, and accompanied Irish nobles to war.*

## People out, wolves in

Europe's wolves have survived in remote areas, especially in mountains and forests. In many parts of Europe, sheep, goats and cattle tend to be kept in fields or mountain meadows rather than (as in North America) on vast expanses of grassland that are hard to patrol. Since the 1950s, Europeans have abandoned their small farms in the mountains and rural areas for the towns. This decrease in the number of farmers has reduced the conflict with wolves.

Europeans have become more enthusiastic about nature and **conservation** – and the wolf – than they used to be. **European Union** laws protect the wolf as an **endangered species**. Since 1989, the Worldwide Fund for Nature has set up the Large **Carnivore** Initiative for Europe (LCIE) to explore people's attitudes to large carnivores, such as wolves, lynx, **wolverines** and bears.

### The Irish wolfhound

In the 17th century, Ireland had so many wolves it was called Wolf-land. The bounty for killing a wolf was £6 – a lot of money in those days. Wolf hunting was a popular sport among the nobility, who used a special kind of greyhound – the Irish wolfhound – to outrun and kill wolves. The earliest record of an Irish wolfhound dates from Roman times, in AD 391. The wolfhound is the tallest breed of dog, measuring 80 centimetres (31 inches) at the shoulder. It has keen eyesight and great strength.

Wolves are reinhabiting many of the areas from which they were once eliminated. They are moving back into Norway and Sweden from Finland. Since gaining partial protection in 1971, Italian wolf numbers are rising, and wolves have spread across the border into France, the Alps (including the Mercantour National Park), and into Switzerland and the Pyrenees. Wolves have been increasing in Poland since the 1950s and are moving out into adjacent countries. With wolves making a comeback in Europe on their own, there are no major plans for reintroductions.

*The Mexican wolf (shown above in a reserve) is a small subspecies of grey wolf. It probably became extinct in the wild around 1980, but was saved by captive breeding, though numbers are still very small.*

Wolves need a huge area of unspoiled wilderness in which to find enough prey. Russia and Canada still have plenty of suitable **habitats** left, but elsewhere some wolf subspecies (for example, the red wolf and Mexican wolf) are dying out. Even in countries with large wilderness areas, wolf prey is often hunted almost to **extinction**, and wolves are driven to prey on livestock or supplement their diet with rubbish. Captive breeding and reintroduction schemes only work if there are suitable areas with enough prey for wolves released into the wild.

It is also vital for the public to be on the side of the wolf for schemes like this to work. Television programmes and the excellent coverage provided by many nature magazines have all helped. Wolf refuges, where people can join in public howls or see wolves and hear talks about them, also boost public awareness of wolves and their needs.

## Keeping the wolves out

Even today, wherever wolves are making a comeback, there is conflict with farmers. French farmers are not at all pleased with the recent arrivals from Italy. Although the government compensates the farmer for the loss of his or her sheep, there is the inconvenience of having to buy more stock. Losses are more of a problem today because farming practice has changed. In the past, shepherds and their dogs stayed with their sheep and goats on the hills, bringing them into safer pens closer to the farmhouse at night. In many parts of Europe today livestock are left in the fields alone and unprotected. In Spain, loss of sheep to wolves is ten times higher in the mountains, where livestock is left to roam, than in the valleys, where they are brought into enclosures at night. Farmers need very strong, high fences to keep out determined wolves, although electric fencing has proved helpful.

## Guard dogs

In some mountainous parts of Europe, dogs are used to guard sheep and goats. When wolves meet dogs, they usually do not try to attack them, and may even greet them like other wolves. As puppies, sheep-guarding dogs are reared with lambs, and form social bonds with the sheep. They are trained not to attack livestock, but to protect the animals from **predators**.

In some parts of Europe, shepherds have bred special dogs to guard their sheep. In the Pyrenees, small dogs called Labrits herd the sheep into a corner of a valley at night, where large Pyrenean mountain dogs keep watch for wolves. Long ago these guard dogs were fitted with wide collars covered in sharp spikes, and in areas where bears were a threat, they might even have had spike-covered body armour. In some places, shepherds used to walk on stilts so that they could spot wolves approaching in the distance. Today in Italy, the Worldwide Fund for Nature is training a traditional sheep-guarding breed, the Abruzzo mastiff, and supplying these dogs to farmers.

A dog guards a flock of sheep in the Tolfa mountains in Italy. Such dogs have been bred and specially trained to defend the flock against attack by wolves.

It is surprising how much just one person can do to help a threatened species. Many rescue schemes have succeeded because of the inspiration and determination of one person. One of the most important things you can do to help the wolf is to spread the word about its needs and put people right about some misguided ideas they may have about it. Collect some nice pictures of wolves to get your friends interested. Persuade your teachers to do a project about wolves.

You can become well informed by reading books about wolves and by looking at websites about them on the Internet. Watch out for programmes about wolves, which will be listed in your television and radio schedules. See if your local nature club offers talks about wolves. If it doesn't, suggest it provide some.

## Adopt a wolf

Several wolf charities have schemes where you can adopt a wolf. You pay a regular small amount of money that helps the charity's work, and in return you receive pictures and information about a particular wolf in their care – 'your wolf'. You may even get the chance to meet your wolf.

If you are lucky enough to have a wolf refuge or zoo near you (or can visit one on holiday), go to see wolves for yourself. Look at their fur and admire the many different shades of colour in it. Gaze at those wonderful golden eyes. Watch how effortlessly wolves move. Listen for the different kinds of wolf 'conversation' noises. Join in a public howl. Visit the information centre to see what you can find out about them.

▲ *MacKenzie was the **alpha** female of the Ambassador Pack at Minnesota's International Wolf Centre until her eyesight began to fail with age. She belongs to the Great Plains wolf subspecies, and is a darker colour than most grey wolves.*

If you are not so lucky to have wolves nearby, check out the websites of the numerous wolf refuges and wolf **conservation** charities. Some have free newsletters to keep you up to date with all their latest activities, including how newly reintroduced wolf packs are doing.

## Wolf shopping

Wolf charities often sell fun gifts with pictures of wolves – paperweights, trinkets, T-shirts, postcards, posters, tea towels, and tapes and CDs of wolves – lots of ideas for birthday and Christmas presents for friends and family.

There are many ways you can raise money to help wolves. You could organize a party with a wolf theme and charge your friends a small fee to come. Or have a sponsored walk, or invite someone to give a talk on wolves (making sure you charge an entrance fee, of course). The humble jumble sale is also good fund-raiser. Don't just sit here reading – do something yourself!

### Wolves on the Internet

There are lots of wolves out there on the web. Try searching with 'wolf' or 'wolves' and words like 'conservation', 'reintroduction', 'refuge', 'rescue', 'centre' and so on. Some wolf conservation groups have regular e-newsletters. Others keep online diaries about wolves they are looking after or about packs that have been reintroduced to new areas. Start with some of the sites listed at the end of this book.

*Wolf adoption kits include specific information about the wolf you have chosen.*

# Glossary

**adaptability**  ability to alter behaviour or structure to cope with changing circumstances, such as the environment, weather or availability of particular types of prey

**alpha**  refers to the dominant pair (having the highest rank) of wolves in a pack, called the alpha male and alpha female

**arthritis**  inflammation of the joints

**billion**  one thousand million

**canine parvovirus**  highly contagious disease of dogs and their relatives, which causes loss of energy and appetite, diarrhoea, vomiting, and sometimes death

**carnivore**  flesh-eating animal

**cattle drive**  long-distance movement of cattle, guided and driven on by men on horseback (cowboys)

**conservation**  management of wild animals, plants and other natural resources to ensure their survival in the future

**conservation legislation**  laws that aim to protect the environment, ensure the survival of endangered  threatened species and habitats, or maintain environmental quality (e.g. freedom from pollution)

**distemper**  highly contagious viral disease of certain mammals

**eco-tourism**  tourism for people interested in wild parts of the world

**endangered species**  species in serious danger of becoming extinct

**European Union**  international organization that includes many of the countries of western Europe and some eastern European countries. It aims to increase trade and work towards common policies in security, domestic and foreign affairs.

**extinct**  no longer existing

**extinction**  decline and eventual total disappearance of a species or subspecies

**flanks**  fleshy parts of side of the body between the ribs and the hip

**flukes**  worm-like animals that live as parasites on other animals

**gangrene**  rotting and death of animal tissues caused by loss of blood supply as a result of injury or infection

**genetic**  relating to inherited information stored in body's cells, which helps to programme much of the body's features and functioning

**genus**   group of closely related species

**habitat**   place where a particular organism lives

**hookworms**   small blood-sucking worms that live as parasites in the intestines of other animals

**hybrid**   organism that is the offspring of two different (but usually closely related) species that have bred together

**mange**   contagious skin disease of animals caused by mites

**migrants**   people who move from one place to another

**migration**   the act of moving from one place to another

**nomads**   people who move from place to place to find pasture and food

**Nordic**   of, or relating to, Scandinavia

**persecute**   to maltreat or, in the case of the wolf throughout history, to eliminate (kill)

**prairies**   extensive stretches of level or rolling uncultivated grassland in North America

**predator**   animal that hunts and kills other animals (prey) to eat

**rabid**   suffering from rabies

**ranchers**   people who own or work on a ranch – a large farm where livestock are reared

**rut**   energetic courtship rituals and fights between deer

**saiga antelope**   pale-coloured hoofed mammal about 76 cm (30 inches) tall at the shoulder, which lives on the steppe grasslands of eastern Europe, Russia and Asia

**steppes**   large stretches of level, treeless grassland found in the drier parts of south-eastern Europe, Russia and Asia

**strychnine**   poison used mainly to kill mice and rats

**tundra**   type of vegetation found in high latitudes and on high mountain tops, which consists of low-growing shrubby plants, grasses, sedges, rushes, mosses and lichens, but no trees

**wolverine**   a powerfully built member of the weasel family that looks like a small bear

# Useful contacts and further reading

## Conservation groups and websites

### USA

**Defenders of Wildlife**
1244 19th Street NW
Washington DC 20036

**The International Wolf Center**
*http://www.wolf.org*
1396 Highway 169
Ely, Minnesota 55731

**The Red Wolf Fund**
Tacoma Zoological Society
5400 North Pearl Street
Tacoma, Washington 98407

**Wolf Haven International**
*http://www.wildwolf.org/*
3111 Offut Lake Road
Tenino, Washington 98589

**Mission: Wolf**
*http://www.missionwolf.com/*
P.O. Box 211
Silver Cliff, Colorado 81249

**Wolf Education Fund**
Zion Natural History Association
Springdale, Utah 84767

**Isle Royale Wolf-Moose Study**
Michigan Tech Fund/Alumni House
Michigan Technical University
Houghton, Michigan 49931

**Mexican Wolf Coalition of New Mexico**
7239 Isleta Boulevard SW
Albuquerque, New Mexico 87105

**Wolf!**
Box 29, Lafayette, Indiana 47902

**Wolf Ecology Project**
School of Forestry
University of Montana
Missoula, Montana 59812

### EUROPE

**Grupo Lobo (Iberian wolf)**
*http://www.timberwolfinformation.org/info/world/grupolobo.htm*
Faculdade de Ciencias
Bloco C2 – Camplo Grande
1700 Lisboa, Portugal

**The Wolf Society of Great Britain**
*http://www.wolfsociety.org.uk*
2 Blackrod Cottages,
Compton Durville, South
Petherton, Somerset, TA13 5EX, UK

## Useful information sites

*http://wildworldofwolves.tripod.com/*
Wild World of Wolves – lots of information and pictures.

*www.nwf.org/wolves*
National Wildlife Federation e-mail newsletter.

*www.searchingwolf.com/ws.htm*
The Searching Wolf lists vast numbers of websites on wolves.

*http://www.wolftrust.org.uk*
The website of the Wolf Trust in the UK.

## Books

*A Society of Wolves: National Parks and the Battle over the Wolf,*
Rick McIntyre (Voyageur Press and Airlife Publishing, 1996)
*Child of the Wolves,* Elizabeth Hall (Yearling Books, 1997)
*Living in a Pack: Wolves,* Richard and Louise Spilsbury
(Heinemann Library, 2003)
*Never Cry Wolf: The Amazing True Story of Life Among Arctic Wolves,*
Farley Mowat (Back Bay Books/Little, Brown & Co., 2001)
*Of Wolves and Men,* Barry Holstun Lopez (Touchstone Books/Simon &
Schuster 1995)
*The Wolf Almanac: A Celebration of Wolves Around the World,*
Robert H. Busch (The Lyons Press, 1998)
*Wolf Songs: The Classic Collection of Writing About Wolves,* ed. Robert
Busch (University of California Press, 1997)
*The World of the Wolf,* Ian Redman (Savage Freedom: Wolf Help, 1988)
*Wolves,* Elizabeth J. Scholl (Kidhaven, 2003)
*Wolves and Other Dogs,* Andrew Solway (Heinemann Library, 2004)
*Wolves: Behavior, Ecology, and Conservation,* eds. David L. Mech and
Luigi Boitani (Chicago University Press, 2003)

## Videos, DVDs and Audio

*Wolves: A Legend Returns to Yellowstone* (National Geographic, 1999)
*Wolf: The Legendary Outlaw* (BBC Video, 1998)
*Wolves at Our Door* (Artisan Entertainment)
*Wailing Wolves/Loups en Liberte* (Natural History Book Service –
www.nhbs.co.uk)

# Index